TOOLS FOR TEACHERS

- **ATOS:** 0.7
- **GRL:** C
- **WORD COUNT:** 34

- **CURRICULUM CONNECTIONS:** weather

Skills to Teach

- **HIGH-FREQUENCY WORDS:** do, is, it, on, that, the, they, will, you
- **CONTENT WORDS:** blows, feel, flag, grow, hold, leaves, moves, seeds, strong, wind(y)
- **PUNCTUATION:** exclamation point, periods, question mark
- **WORD STUDY:** long /e/, spelled ee (feel, seeds), spelled y (windy); long /o/, spelled ow (blows); irregular plural (leaves)
- **TEXT TYPE:** explanation

Before Reading Activities

- Read the title and give a simple statement of the main idea.
- Have students "walk" though the book and talk about what they see in the pictures.
- Introduce new vocabulary by having students predict the first letter and locate the word in the text.
- Discuss any unfamiliar concepts that are in the text.

After Reading Activities

The text mentions how wind moves objects. Explain to children that we cannot see wind. But it can be powerful. Sometimes it is a light breeze. Other times, strong winds can be dangerous. How can winds help? How could they be harmful? Discuss the answers as a group.

Tadpole Books are published by Jump!, 5357 Penn Avenue South, Minneapolis, MN 55419, www.jumplibrary.com

Copyright ©2019 Jump. International copyright reserved in all countries. No part of this book may be reproduced in any form without written permission from the publisher.

Editor: Jenna Trnka **Designer:** Anna Peterson

Photo Credits: Larissa Veronesi/Getty, cover; Nattapon B/Shutterstock, 1; Secheltgirl/Shutterstock, 2–3, 16tl; robinimages2013/Shutterstock, 4–5, 16br; borchee/iStock, 6–7, 16tr; dpetrakov/iStock, 8–9, 16tm; picturepartners/Shutterstock, 10 (dandelions); David Carillet/Shutterstock, 10 (seeds), 16bl; Lopatin Anton/Shutterstock, 11; Photobank gallery/Shutterstock, 12–13, 16bm; bartzuza/Shutterstock, 14–15.

Library of Congress Cataloging-in-Publication Data
Names: Kenan, Tessa, author.
Title: Windy / by Tessa Kenan.
Description: Minneapolis, MN : Jump!, Inc., (2018) | Series: Weather report
Identifiers: LCCN 2017061693 (print) | LCCN 2018001188 (ebook) | ISBN 9781641280143 (ebook) | ISBN 9781641280129 (hardcover : alk. paper) | ISBN 9781641280136 (pbk.)
Subjects: LCSH: Winds—Juvenile literature. | Weather—Juvenile literature.
Classification: LCC QC931.4 (ebook) | LCC QC931.4 .K46 2018 (print) | DDC 551.51/8—dc23
LC record available at https://lccn.loc.gov/2017061693

WEATHER REPORT

WINDY

by Tessa Kenan

TABLE OF CONTENTS

tadpole
books

Do you feel that?

It is windy.

Wind blows.

It moves the leaves.

Wind blows.

flag

It moves the flag.

seed ····▶

Wind blows seeds.

They will grow.

Wind blows.

The wind is strong.

Hold on!

WORDS TO KNOW

feel

flag

leaves

seeds

strong

windy

INDEX